NELSON MANDELA

QUOTES COLLECTION

100+ SELECTED QUOTES

-

CREATED BY:
QUOTES METAVERSE

Nelson Mandela - Quotes Collection - 100+ Selected Quotes
By Quotes Metaverse

Author: Quotes Metaverse
Contact: contact@quotesmetaverse.com

CONTENT

ABOUT NELSON MANDELA

Nelson Rolihlahla Mandela (/mæn'dɛlə/; Xhosa: [xolíɬaɬa mandɛ̂ːla]; 18 July 1918 – 5 December 2013) was a South African anti-apartheid revolutionary, statesman and philanthropist who served as President of South Africa from 1994 to 1999. He was the country's first black head of state and the first elected in a fully representative democratic election. His government focused on dismantling the legacy of apartheid by tackling institutionalised racism and fostering racial reconciliation. Ideologically an African nationalist and socialist, he served as the president of the African National Congress (ANC) party from 1991 to 1997.

A Xhosa speaker, Mandela was born into the Thembu royal family in Mvezo, Union of South Africa. He studied law at the University of Fort Hare and the University of Witwatersrand before working as a lawyer in Johannesburg. There he became involved in anti-colonial and African nationalist politics, joining the ANC in 1943 and co-founding its Youth League in 1944. After the National Party's white-only government established apartheid, a system of racial segregation that privileged whites, Mandela and the ANC committed themselves to its overthrow. He was appointed president of the ANC's Transvaal branch, rising to prominence for his involvement in the 1952 Defiance Campaign and the 1955 Congress of the People. He was repeatedly arrested for seditious activities and was unsuccessfully prosecuted in the 1956 Treason Trial.

Influenced by Marxism, he secretly joined the banned South African Communist Party (SACP). Although initially committed to non-violent protest, in association with the SACP he co-founded the militant Umkhonto we Sizwe in 1961 and led a sabotage campaign against the government. He was arrested and imprisoned in 1962, and subsequently sentenced to life imprisonment for conspiring to overthrow the state following the Rivonia Trial.

Mandela served 27 years in prison, split between Robben Island, Pollsmoor Prison and Victor Verster Prison. Amid growing domestic and international pressure and fears of racial civil war, President F. W. de Klerk released him in 1990. Mandela and de Klerk led efforts to negotiate an end to apartheid, which resulted in the 1994 multiracial general election in which Mandela led the ANC to victory and became president. Leading a broad coalition government which promulgated a new constitution, Mandela emphasised reconciliation between the country's racial groups and created the Truth and Reconciliation Commission to investigate past human rights abuses. Economically, his administration retained its predecessor's liberal framework despite his own socialist beliefs, also introducing measures to encourage land reform, combat poverty and expand healthcare services. Internationally, Mandela acted as mediator in the Pan Am Flight 103 bombing trial and served as secretary-general of the Non-Aligned Movement from 1998 to 1999.

He declined a second presidential term and was succeeded by his deputy, Thabo Mbeki. Mandela became an elder statesman and focused on combating poverty and HIV/AIDS through the charitable Nelson Mandela Foundation.

Mandela was a controversial figure for much of his life. Although critics on the right denounced him as a communist terrorist and those on the far left deemed him too eager to negotiate and reconcile with apartheid's supporters, he gained international acclaim for his activism. Widely regarded as an icon of democracy and social justice, he received more than 250 honours, including the Nobel Peace Prize. He is held in deep respect within South Africa, where he is often referred to by his Thembu clan name, Madiba, and described as the "Father of the Nation".

BASIC INFORMATION

1st President of South Africa
In office: 10 May 1994 – 16 June 1999
Deputy:
Thabo Mbeki
F. W. de Klerk
Preceded by: F. W. de Klerk (State Pres.)
Succeeded by: Thabo Mbeki

11th President of the African National Congress
In office: 7 July 1991 – 20 December 1997
Deputy:
Walter Sisulu
Thabo Mbeki
Preceded by: Oliver Tambo
Succeeded by: Thabo Mbeki

19th Secretary General of the Non-Aligned Movement
In office: 2 September 1998 – 16 June 1999
Preceded by: Andrés Pastrana Arango
Succeeded by: Thabo Mbeki

Personal details
Born: Rolihlahla Mandela
18 July 1918
Mvezo, Cape Province, Union of South Africa (now Eastern Cape)

Died: 5 December 2013 (aged 95)
Johannesburg, Gauteng, Republic of South Africa

Resting place: Mandela Graveyard
Qunu, Eastern Cape, South Africa

Political party: African National Congress

Other political affiliations: South African Communist

Spouse(s):
Evelyn Ntoko Mase (m. 1944; div. 1958)
Winnie Madikizela (m. 1958; div. 1996)
Graça Machel (m. 1998)

Children: 7, including Makgatho, Makaziwe, Zenani, Zindziswa and Josina (step-daughter)

Parents:
Nosekeni Fanny (mother)
Gadla Henry Mphakanyiswa (father)

Alma mater:
University of Fort Hare
University of London
University of South Africa
University of the Witwatersrand

Occupation:
Activist, politician, philanthropist, lawyer

Known for: Internal resistance to apartheid

Awards:
Sakharov Prize (1988)
Bharat Ratna (1990)
Nishan-e-Pakistan (1992)
Nobel Peace Prize (1993)
Lenin Peace Prize (1990)
Presidential Medal of Freedom (2002)

Nickname(s):
Madiba. Dalibunga

Writing career
Notable works: Long Walk to Freedom

NELSON MANDELA QUOTES

-

"There can be no greater gift than that of giving one's time and energy to help others without expecting anything in return".

—

"No one is born hating another person because of the color of his skin, or his background, or his religion. People must learn to hate, and if they can learn to hate, they can be taught to love, for love comes more naturally to the human heart than its opposite."

—

"I learned that courage was not the absence of fear, but the triumph over it. The brave man is not he who does not feel afraid, but he who conquers that fear."

—

"Do not judge me by my success, judge me by how many times I fell down and got back up again."

—

"It only seems impossible until it's done."

—

"Fools multiply when wise men are silent."

—

"Education is the great engine of personal development. It is through education that the daughter of a peasant can become a doctor, that the son of a mineworker can become the head of the mine, that a child of farm workers can become the president of a great nation. It is what we make out of what we have, not what we are given, that separates one person from another."

—

"What counts in life is not the mere fact that we have lived. It is what difference we have made to the lives of others that will determine the significance of the life we lead."

—

"Education is the most powerful weapon which you can use to change the world."

—

"If you want the cooperation of humans around you, you must make them feel they are important - and you do that by being genuine and humble."

—

"A winner is a dreamer who never gives up."

—

"May your choices reflect your hopes, not your fears."

—

"Like slavery and apartheid, poverty is not natural. It is man-made and it can be overcome and eradicated by the actions of human beings."

—

"Freedom can never be taken for granted. Each generation must safeguard it and extend it. Your parents and elders sacrificed much so that you should have freedom without suffering what they did. Use this precious right to ensure that the darkness of the past never returns."

—

"Everyone can rise above their circumstances and achieve success if they are dedicated to and passionate about what they do."

—

"When we dehumanise and demonise our opponents, we abandon the possibility of peacefully resolving our differences, and seek to justify violence against them."

—

"When a man is denied the right to live the life he believes in, he has no choice but to become an outlaw."

—

"You can start changing our world for the better daily, no matter how small the action."

—

"In Africa there is a concept known as 'ubuntu' - the profound sense that we are human only through the humanity of others; that if we are to accomplish anything in this world it will in equal measure be due to the work and achievement of others."

—

"It is so easy to break down and destroy. The heroes are those who make peace and build."

—

"My dream would be a multicultural society, one that is diverse and where every man, woman and child are treated equally. I dream of a world where all people of all races work together in harmony."

—

"Live life as though nobody is watching, and express yourself as though everyone is listening."

—

"In judging our progress as individuals we tend to concentrate on external factors such as one's social position, influence and popularity, wealth and standard of education... But internal factors may be even more crucial in assessing one's development as a human being. Honesty, sincerity, simplicity, humility, pure generosity, absence of vanity, readiness to serve others - qualities which are within easy reach of every soul - are the foundation of one's spiritual life."

—

"Forgiveness liberates the soul. It removes fear. That is why it is such a powerful weapon."

—

"Lead from the back — and let others believe they are in front."

—

"After climbing a great hill, one only finds that there are many more hills to climb."

—

"If you talk to a man in a language he understands, that goes to his head. If you talk to him in his language, that goes to his heart."

—

"There is no passion to be found playing small - in settling for a life that is less than the one you are capable of living."

—

"One of the most difficult things is not to change society - but to change yourself."

—

"I have walked that long road to freedom. I have tried not to falter; I have made missteps along the way. But I have discovered the secret that after climbing a great hill, one only finds that there are many more hills to climb. I have taken a moment here to rest, to steal a view of the glorious vista that surrounds me, to look back on the distance I have come. But I can only rest for a moment, for with freedom come responsibilities, and I dare not linger, for my long walk is not ended."

—

"It is always impossible until it is done."

—

"As long as poverty, injustice and gross inequality persist in our world, none of us can truly rest."

—

"We know what needs to be done - all that is missing is the will to do it."

—

"A good leader can engage in a debate frankly and thoroughly, knowing that at the end he and the other side must be closer, and thus emerge stronger. You don't have that idea when you are arrogant, superficial, and uninformed."

—

"For to be free is not merely to cast off one's chains, but to live in a way that respects and enhances the freedom of others."

—

"The true character of a society is revealed in how it treats its children."

—

“The past is a rich resource on which we can draw in order to make decisions for the future, but it does not dictate our choices. We should look back at the past and select what is good, and leave behind what is bad.”

—

“As I walked out the door toward the gate that would lead to my freedom, I knew if I didn't leave my bitterness and hatred behind, I'd still be in prison.”

—

“If the ANC does to you what the apartheid government did to you, then you must do to the ANC what you did to the apartheid government.”

—

“There is no future without forgiveness.”

—

“Honour belongs to those who never forsake the truth even when things seem dark and grim, who try over and over again, who are never discouraged by insults, humiliation and even defeat.”

—

“A good head and a good heart are always a formidable combination.”

—

"The brave man is not the one who has no fears, he is the one who triumphs over his fears."

—

"A real leader uses every issue, no matter how serious and sensitive, to ensure that at the end of the debate we should emerge stronger and more united than ever before."

—

"It is what we make out of what we have, not what we are given, that separates one person from another."

—

"It is not where you start but how high you aim that matters for success."

—

"Remember to celebrate milestones as you prepare for the road ahead."

—

"I like friends who have independent minds because they tend to make you see problems from all angles."

—

"A critical, independent and investigative press is the lifeblood of any democracy. The press must be free from state interference. It must have the economic strength to stand up to the blandishments of government officials. It must have sufficient independence from vested interests to be bold and inquiring without fear or favour. It must enjoy the protection of the constitution, so that it can protect our rights as citizens."

—

"The call now is for each of us to ask ourselves: are we doing all we can to help build the country of our dreams?"

—

"Thinking is one of the most important weapons in dealing with problems."

—

"Part of being optimistic is keeping one's head pointed toward the sun, one's feet moving forward."

—

"I learned to have the patience to listen when people put forward their views, even if I think those views are wrong. You can't reach a just decision in a dispute unless you listen to both sides."

—

"There is nothing more important in life than giving. Tolerance is forged when people look beyond their own desires."

—

"Racism is a blight on the human conscience. The idea that any people can be inferior to another, to the point where those who consider themselves superior define and treat the rest as subhuman, denies the humanity even of those who elevate themselves to the status of gods."

—

"Few things make the life of a parent more rewarding and sweet as successful children."

—

"Death is something inevitable. When a man has done what he considers to be his duty to his people and his country, he can rest in peace. I believe I have made that effort and that is, therefore, why I will sleep for the eternity."

—

"You mustn't compromise your principles, but you mustn't humiliate the opposition. No one is more dangerous than one who is humiliated."

—

"Our task is not to liberate the oppressed, but to liberate the oppressors."

—

"A leader. . .is like a shepherd. He stays behind the flock, letting the most nimble go out ahead, whereupon the others follow, not realizing that all along they are being directed from behind."

—

"Appearances matter — and remember to smile."

—

"One cannot be prepared for something while secretly believing it will not happen."

—

"Our fear is not that we are inadequate, but that we are powerful beyond measure."

—

"I had no epiphany, no singular revelation, no moment of truth, but a steady accumulation of a thousand slights, a thousand indignities and a thousand unremembered moments produced in me an anger, a rebelliousness, a desire to fight the system that imprisoned my people. There was no particular day on which I said, Henceforth I will devote myself to the liberation of my people; instead, I simply found myself doing so, and could not do otherwise."

—

"Our children are our greatest treasure. They are our future. Those who abuse them tear at the fabric of our society and weaken our nation."

—

"It is not our diversity which divides us; it is not our ethnicity, or religion or culture that divides us. Since we have achieved our freedom, there can only be one division amongst us: between those who cherish democracy and those who do not."

—

"I am fundamentally an optimist. Whether that comes from nature or nurture, I cannot say. Part of being optimistic is keeping one's head pointed toward the sun, one's feet moving forward. There were many dark moments when my faith in humanity was sorely tested, but I would not and could not give myself up to despair. That way lays defeat and death."

—

"It is not the kings and generals that make history, but the masses of the people."

—

"Peace is the greatest weapon for development that any person can have."

—

"Resentment is like a glass of poison that a man drinks; then he sits down and waits for his enemy to die."

—

"No power on this earth can destroy the thirst for human dignity."

—

"It never hurts to think too highly of a person; often they become ennobled and act better because of it."

—

"No country can really develop unless its citizens are educated."

—

"Safety and security don't just happen, they are the result of collective consensus and public investment. We owe our children, the most vulnerable citizens in our society, a life free of violence and fear."

—

"Overcoming poverty is not a gesture of charity. It is an act of justice. It is the protection of a fundamental human right, the right to dignity and a decent life . .

—

"The day I am afraid to do, that is the day I am no longer fit to lead."

—

"Blaming things on the past does not make them better."

—

"Sports have the power to change the world. It has the power to inspire, the power to unite people in a way that little else does. It speaks to youth in a language they understand. Sports can create hope, where there was once only despair. It is more powerful than governments in breaking down racial barriers. It laughs in the face of all types of discrimination. Sports is the game of lovers."

—

"We must use time wisely and forever realize that the time is always ripe to do right."

—

"Where you stand depends on where you sit."

—

"Those who conduct themselves with morality, integrity and consistency need not fear the forces of inhumanity and cruelty."

—

"We know it well that none of us acting alone can achieve success."

—

"Artists reach areas far beyond the reach of politicians. Art, especially entertainment and music, is understood by everybody, and it lifts the spirits and the morale of those who hear it."

—

"Great anger and violence can never build a nation."

—

"Courage is not the absence of fear — it s inspiring others to move beyond it."

—

"Political division, based on color, is entirely artificial; and when it disappears, so will the domination of one color group by another."

—

"There is no easy walk to freedom anywhere."

—

"Great peacemakers are all people of integrity, of honesty, but humility."

—

"People respond in accordance to how you relate to them. If you approach them on the basis of violence, that's how they'll react. But if you say, 'We want peace, we want stability,' we can then do a lot of things that will contribute towards the progress of our society."

—

"For every woman and girl violently attacked, we reduce our humanity. For every woman forced into unprotected sex because men demand this, we destroy dignity and pride. Every woman who has to sell her life for sex we condemn to a lifetime in prison. For every moment we remain silent, we conspire against our women. For every woman infected by HIV, we destroy a generation."

—

"Exercise is the key not only to physical health but to peace of mind."

—

"The best weapon is to sit down and talk."

—

"Hope is a powerful weapon, and (one) no one power on earth can deprive you of."

—

"Rhetoric is not important. Actions are."

—

"Take it upon yourself where you live to make people around you joyful and full of hope."

—

"The very right to be human is denied every day to hundreds of millions of people as a result of poverty, the unavailability of basic necessities such as food, jobs, water and shelter, education, health care and a healthy environment."

—

"Nothing is black or white."

—

"Freedom is meaningless if people cannot put food in their stomachs, if they can have no shelter, if illiteracy and disease continue to dog them."

—

"The time has come to accept in our hearts and minds that with freedom comes responsibility."

—

"Man's goodness is a flame that can be hidden but never extinguished."

NELSON MANDELA

QUOTES COLLECTION

100+ SELECTED QUOTES

NOTE ABOUT THE BOOK

As the reader has been able to perceive, this book has specific elements in its content that serve as motivation and inspiration to apply in their daily life, so I suggest its periodic reading, in such a way to internalize the concepts and in this way to convert them into habits of daily use.

REVIEWS

Thank you for having read this book, we hope that its content has been useful and will serve to deepen your knowledge on the person. If you really liked the book, we thank you for leaving me a sincere review.

The best way for new authors, as is our case, to stand out and get the better positioning of their books is through positive reviews. That way we can continue writing, besides being able to improve the quality day by day.

Thank you very much!

LEGAL DISCLAIMER

This book aims to provide information and entertainment to its readers. Its content is based on sources considered reliable, however, the author cannot confirm or guarantee its accuracy and validity and is not responsible for any error or omission. In no case, the reader must assume the contents of this book as professional advice, nor does it intend to substitute the functions of the experts in the area, therefore, it is a guide whose application should be consulted with the professionals accredited in the area before being used. In the case of protocols or medical treatments described in the contents of this book, the reader must receive qualified professional medical advice before using any of the resources or techniques described in this book.

The reader agrees to accept that by using the information contained in this book, the author is exempt from liability for costs, expenses, damages, and even professional fees that may arise from the application of any detail described in this book. This disclaimer applies even to the direct or indirect application of any information presented, whether due to a breach of contract, grievance, negligence, personal injury, criminal intent or under any other cause of action.

COPYRIGHT

Nelson Mandela - Quotes Collection - 100+ Selected Quotes
By Quotes Metaverse

Author: Quotes Metaverse
Contact: contact@quotesmetaverse.com

www.ingramcontent.com/pod-product-compliance
Ingram Content Group UK Ltd.
Pitfield, Milton Keynes, MK11 3LW, UK
UKHW022009190726
13853UKWH00004B/1825